11

I hope you'll keep this forever.

I would love for these words to be
here for you all your lives, helping
you realize that each one of you
will always be a wonderful gift,
    a treasure of memories, and
        an amazing miracle to me.

ISBN: 0-88396-677-8

Dedication: For Jordan and Casey

Manufactured in China.
First Printing: June 2002

 This book is printed on recycled paper.
This book is printed on fine quality, laid embossed, 80 lb. paper. This paper has been specially produced to be acid free (neutral pH) and contains no groundwood or unbleached pulp. It conforms with all the requirements of the American National Standards Institute, Inc., so as to ensure that this book will last and be enjoyed by future generations.

SPS Studios, Inc.
P.O. Box 4549, Boulder, Colorado 80306

A Keepsake for
MY CHILDREN

A special book I'm going to give to
each one of you, with the hope that
you'll hold on to these thoughts forever

by Douglas Pagels

Blue Mountain Press™
SPS Studios, Inc., Boulder, Colorado

A Keepsake for My Children

There is never a day that goes by without my thinking of what beautiful blessings you are to my life. God must have been smiling down on me... when you came into the world. And I promise you this: it would be a far less fantastic, rewarding, and remarkable place... without you.

I am so enormously proud of each one of you! I love you beyond all words that I will ever be able to say, and I will love you every moment, every day of my life...

There are gifts that are far above
　　priceless.
There are memories that are
　　made of pure love.
There are special miracles that
　　really do come true.

And all my life, each one of
　　you will always be...
a wonderful gift, a treasure of
　　memories, and an amazing
　　miracle... to me.

"For My Children"
Words I Want You to Remember

I can barely begin to tell you of all my wishes for each of you • There are so many of them, and I want them all to come true • I want you to use your heart as a compass as you grow and find your way in the world, but I want you to always have an appreciation for the direction of home • I want you to be self-reliant, self-motivated, and self-sufficient, but to know that you will never be alone • I want you to be safe and smart and cautious • I want you to be wise beyond your years • I don't want you to grow up too fast • I want you to come to me with your fears…

For you, my children: I want the people who share your days to realize that they are in the presence of a very special someone ✦ You are a wonderful, rare person with no comparison ✦ I want you to know that opportunities will come, and you'll have many goals to achieve ✦ The more that obstacles get in the way of your dreams, the more you'll need to believe...

I want you to remember to get your feet wet with new experiences, but be sure you never get in over your head ✴ I want you to realize how capable you are and that your possibilities are unlimited ✴ I hope you never lose your childlike wonder, your delight and appreciation in interesting things ✴ I know you'll keep responding in a positive way to the challenges life always brings ✴ I pray that you won't rush the future and that you'll slowly build on the steppingstones of the past ✴ You have a strong foundation of family and friends and joy that will always last…

I wish I could find the words to tell you how much
I love you each and every day • But that feeling
is so strong and its meaning is so magnificent, it
    can be hard to know just what to say •

I love you beyond all words • And I promise that
I will love you beyond all time • So many treasures
await you in your journey of life…

    and being blessed with you… has been mine •

I Wish for You...

Happiness. Deep down within.
Serenity. With each sunrise.
Success. In each facet of your life.
Close and caring friends.
Love. That never ends.

Special memories. Of all the yesterdays.
A bright today. With much to
be thankful for.
A path. That leads to beautiful tomorrows.

Dreams. That do their best to come true.
And appreciation. Of all the wonderful
things about you.

Sometimes we need
reminders in our lives
of how much people care.

If you ever get that feeling,
    I want you to remember this…

Beyond words that can even begin
to tell you how much,
I hold you and your happiness
within my heart each and
    every day.

I am so proud of you and so thankful
to the years that have given me
so much to be thankful for.

Poems to Help My Children Be Strong
Along the Path of Life

"You've got so many possibilities ahead! Don't be
too quick to limit your choices of what to do, because
you might limit your chances of unimagined joys that
are waiting just for you."

> "Always keep your goodness
> and never lose your love.
> For then you'll be
> rewarded with success
> in ways you never dreamed of."

"In the course of time, you will be reminded
that hard work gets good results and keeping
healthy is essential. Know when to work your mind
and let your body relax, and know when doing just
the opposite makes the most sense. Being able
to handle whatever life brings your way
is not a matter of coincidence."

"You've got a wonderful sense of
humor and a good outlook on life.
Let those qualities help to see you
through when you're deciding where to
go and you're not sure what to do."

"One of the best things you can accomplish on life's
pathway is to be a walking example of the golden
rule. Don't let anyone fool you into thinking that
it is worthless; it is one of the most valuable things
you can do."

"You've got a big heart. Keep it filled with happiness.
You've got a fascinating mind. Keep finding new ways
to grow. Keep yearning. Keep learning. Keep trying.
Keep smiling. And keep remembering that a parent's
love goes with you… everywhere you go."

To have a child
is to be given
the world to hold
in your hands...

And the entire universe
to try to fit
inside your heart.

My child, when you came into this world and into my life, so many beautiful things happened. Although I was the one holding you, you were the one enfolding so many of my hopes and dreams. Although I was the one who was supposed to teach you all the things to do as you grew up, you were the one who taught me — constantly — of my capacity to love, to experience life in its most meaningful way, and to open my heart wide enough to let all those joyful feelings inside.

The Way You Are

I just want you to take a while to read this.
I know your days are busy, but I hope they
are giving back to you as much as you give
to them.

And I know there are moments when things
could be better, but I hope you'll remember
that good things come to good people and
that — without a doubt — you are one of
the best. There are so many wonderful things
about you. But I think that the most admirable
thing of all, at least to me, is that you do the
things you do with an inner strength and a
special kind of love. That's just the way
you are.

You give life a gleam that most people only
carry a glimpse of.

If I could have any wish I wanted,
   this would be my wish...

That in your life,
   which is so precious to me,
may troubles, worries, and problems
never linger;
may they only make you
that much stronger and able
and wise.

And may you rise each day with
sunlight in your heart,
success in your path,
answers to your prayers, and
that smile — that I love to see —
   always there... in your eyes.

"Never"

Don't ever try to understand everything; some things will just never make sense • Don't ever be afraid to try to make things better; you might be surprised at the results • Don't ever feel threatened by the future; enjoy life one day at a time • Don't ever feel guilty about the past; simply learn from any mistakes that were made • Don't ever feel that you are alone; there is always somebody there for you to reach out to • Don't ever forget that you can achieve so many of the things you can imagine; it's not as hard as it seems • Don't ever stop loving • Don't ever stop believing • Don't ever stop dreaming your dreams •

"Always"

Make your tomorrows everything you want them to be ✦ If there is a change to be made, set the stage for tomorrow to bring it ✦ When you're not sure what to do, trust your intuition and just wing it ✦ When in doubt, you would be wise to listen to the lesson of a tree: live your life with your own personal sense of majesty ✦ Let the roots of all your dreams grow deep ✦ Let the hopes of all your tomorrows grow high ✦ Bend, but don't break ✦ Take the seasons as they come ✦
    Stick up for yourself ✦
        And reach for the sky ✦

Each Day

Each day is a blank page in the diary of your life. And there is something special you need to remember in order to turn your life story into the treasure it deserves to be.

This is how it works...

Follow your dreams. Work hard. Be kind. This is all anyone could ever ask: Do what you can to make the door open on a day that is filled with inspiration in some special way.

Remember: Goodness will be rewarded. Smiles will pay you back. Have fun. Find strength. Be truthful. Have faith. Don't focus on anything you lack.

Realize that people are the treasures in life, and happiness is the real wealth. Have a diary that describes how you are doing your best, and...

The rest will take care of itself.

One of the secrets of happiness is to take time to accomplish what you have to do, then to make time to achieve what you want to do.

Remember that life is short. Its golden moments need hopes and memories and dreams. When it seems like those things are lost in the shuffle, you owe it to yourself to find them again. The days are too precious to let them slip away. If you're working too hard, make sure it's because it's a sacrifice for a time when you're going to pay yourself back with something more important than ordinary things could ever be. If you're losing the battle, do what it takes to win the war over who is in control of your destiny.

Find time, make time, take time... to do something rewarding and deeply personal and completely worthwhile. Time is your fortune, and you can spend it to bring more joy to yourself and to others your whole life through.

Time is your treasure. And instead of working too hard for it, do what it takes to make it work...
for you.

Today you have been given twenty-four
wonderful things: the hours in this day...
to spend in the most beautiful and
meaningful way possible.

Let this day be a reflection of
the strength that resides within you.
Of the courage that lights your path.
Of the wisdom that guides your steps.

And of the serenity that will be yours
when this day has passed.

Live Life in a Beautiful Way

Live to the fullest, and make each day count.
Don't let the important things go unsaid.
Have simple pleasures in this complex world.
Be a joyous spirit and sensitive soul.
Take those long walks that would love to be
taken. Explore those sunlit paths that would
love to oblige. Don't just have minutes in the
day; have moments in time. Believe in the new
strength you're discovering inside.

Make tomorrow happier by going there in
ways that really matter. And don't ever
forget that, eventually… dream-chasers
become dream-catchers.

Keep the promises you promised yourself.
Improve on the things that seemed so difficult
in the beginning. Grow in courage and strength
and be equal to your tasks. Discover new paths
and put disappointment far behind you. And
don't ever make the mistake of giving up on your
faith: There will come a time when you will be so
thankful for having walked through the doors
that led to the life you were searching for.

The world is a wonderful place, but it is
never generous enough to blanket us
with security and to let us live life with
stars in our eyes.

Our optimism is always tempered with
realism. And try as we might to keep
them up, hopes can fade and stars can fall.

But every time I see a falling star,
I'll wish for this:

That you and I will never lose the gleam
that love provides to hearts that continue
to hope for the best...
and very often receive it.

Twelve Ways to Keep Smiling

Hold on to your dreams, and never let them go. Show the rest of the world what so many people already know: how wonderful you are!

Give circumstances a chance, and give others the benefit of the doubt. Wish on a star that shines in your sky. Take on your problems one by one and work things out.

Rely on all the strength you have inside. Let loose of the sparkle and spirit that you sometimes try to hide. Stay in touch with those who touch your life with love...

Look on the bright side and don't let
adversity keep you from winning. Be
yourself, because you are filled with
special qualities that have brought
you this far, and that will always see
you through.

Keep your spirits up. Make your heart
happy, and let it reflect on everything
you do!

Each Step of the Way

May you find happiness in every direction your paths take you. May you never lose that sense of wonder you have always had, and may you hold on to the sense of humor you use to brighten the lives of everyone who knows you. May you go beyond the ordinary steps and discover extraordinary results. May you keep on trying to reach for your stars, and may you never forget how wonderful you are.

May you always be patient with the problems of life, and know that any clouds will eventually give way to the sunlight of your most hoped-for days. May you be rewarded with the type of friendships that get better and better — and the kind of love that blesses your life forever.

May you hold on to your dreams and keep them safe in your heart. May you go out of your way to stay healthy in body and soul, and may you know what it takes to deal with the stress of living in what is sometimes a difficult world...

May you never lose your ability to see your way through to the other side of any worries. May you share your beautiful spirit with others, and remember how much magic a smile can provide.

May you meet every challenge you are faced with, recognize every precious opportunity, and be blessed with the knowledge that you have the ability to make every day special. May you have enough material wealth to meet your needs, while never forgetting that the real treasures of life are the loved ones and friends who are invaluable to the end. May you search for serenity, and discover it was within you all along.

May you be strong enough to keep your hopes and dreams alive. May you always be gentle enough to understand. May you know that you hold tomorrow in your hands, and that every part of the journey ahead brings a chance to make some wonderful memories.

And may you always remember, each step of the way...
You are loved, more than words
can ever say.

It takes a lot to set your sights on a distant horizon and to keep on reaching for your goals. It takes a lot... of courage and hard work, believing and achieving, patience and perseverance, inner strength and gentle hope. It takes a lot of giving it your best and doing the fantastic things you do.

But most of all...

It takes someone as wonderful as you.

I Care So Much
About You

I care about you more than I can say.
And that caring and that feeling
have a meaning that is more precious
and more special to me than
    I can explain.

But let me try to tell you this...

Saying "I care" means that I will always
    do everything I can to understand.
It means that you can trust me.
It means that you can tell me
    what's wrong.
It means that I will try to fix what I can,
that I will listen
when you need me to hear, and that
— even in your most difficult moment —
    all you have to do is say the word,
        and your hand and my hand
            will not be apart.

It means that whenever you speak to me,
whether words are spoken through a smile
    or through a tear...
        I will listen with all my heart.

Rise Above It

There will always be tough times and difficult days in our lives. It seems like some things weren't meant to be, and some plans just weren't meant to work out. There will always be disappointments to deal with, but there will be so many special blessings, too.

All that is asked of any of us is to try and rise above our problems. Let life show you new ways of doing things. Let it bring you new discoveries. Let the days introduce you to possibilities you've never known, to dreams you've never dreamed, and to the seeds of ideas you've never sown before...

Let life help you sweeten your beliefs and show you everything hiding just behind the scenes: the deep peace of the changing seasons; the majesty of what it means to have — and be — a friend; the joy to be found in knowing that it's never too late to begin again. Let life bring abundance into your heart and soul. Let it sing in you and show you how to aim for the stars. Let it help you reach out to be all that you are.

It's a pretty simple rule: The more you give... the more you get back. And the more you do that, the more you'll love it.

You're a wonderful person who deserves to have a beautiful life. And if difficulty ever comes along, I know... that you can rise above it.

You have inspired more pride and you have
reaffirmed more love than most parents'
hearts could even begin to contain.

All of your lives, as each of you grew,
I knew that my heart had to keep
getting bigger and bigger
if it was possibly going to keep up
with all the feelings
      I have for you.

You have an amazing way of touching my heart, and you have a way of turning every day into a time and a place where the nicest feelings and the deepest gratitude all come together.

The next time you're touched by a gentle breeze, it just might be one that I asked, please, to carry my reminder of caring to you.

Every hour, every day, every time you find yourself wondering if anyone may be thinking of you, smile and quietly remember that I am, and I always will be.

You're a Very Special Person

Carry the sun inside you, and reach
out for the dreams that guide you.
You have everything you need to take
you where you want to go. You have
abilities and talents and attributes that
belong to you alone, and you have
what it takes to make your path of
success… lead to happiness.

You're a very special person.
You have qualities that get better every day!
You have the courage and strength to see
    things through.
You have smiles that will serve as your guides.
You have a light that will shine in you 'til the
    end of time…

You have known the truth of yesterday, and
    you have an inner map that will lead the way
    to a very beautiful tomorrow.
You have gifts that have never even been
    opened and personal journeys waiting to be
    explored. You have <u>so</u> <u>much</u> going for you.
You are a special person, and you have a
    future that is in the best of hands. And you
    need to remember: If you have plans you
    want to act on and dreams you've always
    wanted to come true…

        You have what it takes, because…
            You
                have
                    you.

What I Want to Be to You

A place you can come to for comfort.
Eyes you can look at and trust.
A hand you can reach out and clasp.
A heart that understands and doesn't judge.

Someone you can lean on and learn from.
A source of wisdom and loving advice.
A million memories in the making.
A precious companion on the path of life.

A door that is always open.
A caring, gentle hug.
A time that is devoted to family alone.
A lasting reflection of love.

Gifts of the Heart

If I were to tell you all the reasons you mean so much to me, it would take me thousands of words — to convey how proud I am of you, how much you make me smile, and how often you are in my thoughts.

Right before my eyes, you have grown up so much on your way to becoming the special person you are today.

You were always full of life and filled with surprises. Trying to keep up with you has been many things: rewarding, challenging, hopeful, and fulfilling. In every one of your years, you have given me more happiness and love than most people will ever dream of.

As a family, we have walked along many paths on our way from yesterday to where we are today. Love has always been our companion, keeping us close even when we've been apart.

You have given me many gifts on that journey. But none are more precious than the smiles you give to my heart.

Remember that You Can Always Count on Me

When life isn't easy and you wonder if anyone understands what you're going through, I want you… to reach out to me. Even if we find ourselves miles apart, don't ever forget that my heart is filled with so many hopes for your happiness.

I want you to feel like you can tell me everything that's on your mind. I want to be able to help you find a million more smiles and make your days more joyful and filled with all the serenity you so dearly deserve.

When you wonder if there is anyone who
cares completely and unconditionally,
look my way. Let down your guard, and
know that it's okay to bare your soul with
someone who knows you as well as I do.
When you need to talk things out, realize
that you'll find a very loving listener...
in me.

It doesn't matter what it's for; if it's
important to you, then it's important
to me. What matters most is that you
gently remember:
    Sometimes two heads (and two
    hearts) are better than one can
    be, and you can always count
       on me to be there for you.

Promise Me This

Promise me you'll always remember what a special
person you are • Promise me you'll hold on to
your hopes and reach out for your stars •
Promise me you'll live with happiness over the
years and over the miles • Promise me that when
you think of me, it will always be with a smile •
Promise me you'll "remember when..." and you'll
always "look forward to..." • Promise me you'll
do the things you have always wanted to do •
Promise me you'll cherish your dreams as treasures
you have kept • Promise me you'll enjoy life day
by day and step by step • Promise me you'll
always remember the wishes I have for you...

For I wish you
a life of love and joy
and all your dreams
come true.

A Few Words from the Heart

In your happiest and most exciting moments, my
   heart will celebrate and smile beside you.
In your lowest lows, my love will be there to keep
   you warm, to give you strength, and to remind
   you that your sunshine is sure to come again.
In your moments of accomplishment, I will be filled
   so full of pride that I may have a hard time
   keeping the feeling inside of me.
In your moments of disappointment, I will be a
   shoulder to cry on, and a hand to hold, and
   a love that will gently enfold you until
   everything's okay.
In your gray days, I will help you search, one by one,
   for the colors of the rainbow.
In your bright and shining hours, I will be smiling,
   too, right along beside you.

I will care about how the world is treating you
every day of your life.

Don't be afraid to do what you once thought impossible, even if others don't think you'll succeed. Remember that history is filled with the incredible accomplishments of those who were foolish enough...

to believe.

———— ❧ ————

When you're searching for success, do you find it or does it find you? Maybe it's a little of both. You're on the path, your mind is open to the possibilities, your heart is full of hope, and you bump into each other in a way that feels exactly like it was meant to be.

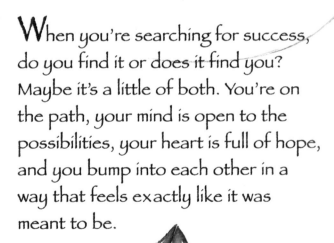

Wonderful Possibilities

A life well lived is simply a
compilation of days well spent.

You can accomplish so much
in all the years ahead
just by making sure that you
try to do at least one
memorable, meaningful,
fun, or fulfilling thing
before the setting of each sun.

And remember that it is easily
within the reach of everyone
to become independently wealthy
in the most gratifying way.

All you have to do...

is treasure

every single day.

A Prayer for Our Family

Please help to make this day and all that follow
a time of togetherness and understanding.
Please help the light of serenity shine in
through an open door, warming the heart
and encouraging the soul.

Please help to chase away any clouds
and lessen any troubles in this day.
Please help to provide the reassurance that hope,
blessings, and a world of beautiful things
are always there if we just take the time to see.
Please help us learn that life goes on, rainbows
return, and the difficulties that inevitably
come to everyone turn into insurmountable
concerns only if we let them...

Please help us realize that problems can only
    impact us to the extent that we give them
    power over our hearts and minds.
Please empower us with patience, faith, and love.

Please help us choose the path we walk instead
    of letting it choose us.
Please let it take us to the brighter day that is
    always there, even though it is not always seen.
Please help us to be wiser than our worries,
    stronger than any situation that can come
    our way, and steadily assured of our beliefs.
Please help us reach the goals that wait for us
    on the horizons that encourage us on.
Please enfold us within each new sunset and
    inspire us with each new dawn.

Our Love

There are some things that can only be understood among family. There are words that only we can say, smiles that only we can inspire, and dreams that can only be shared between people who care... the way we do.

My child, I want you to know how much I appreciate you.

What we share is so essential. We share something that is stronger than any storm, that is wonderful and caring and warm, that is supportive and trusting and sweet.

Our love is something our hearts and our happiness will always treasure and keep.

That's What Love Does

If you have any tough times in the years ahead, when the days aren't going the way you'd like them to, I want you to remember, please: You can always turn to me.

I want to be a place you can come to... for shelter, for unconditional caring, for sharing all the support one person can give. I want to be a person you can turn to... for answers and understanding, or just to reinforce the feeling of how incredibly special you are.

I want to do everything I possibly can for you because that's what love does when it is strong and grateful and giving.

I want you to know what a gift it is
    to be your parent,
        and that my love for you...
            is never-ending.

Problems and predicaments come to us all.
There's no sign saying: "You must be this tall…"
to ride on the emotional roller coasters that
take so many of us for a spin. The bad news is
that there are times when we're passengers…
whether we like it or not. The good news is that
we can always choose to get off at the next stop.

The mantra to always help you make it through:
"Need to, can do. Have to, will do."

You Are So Deserving

You are something — and someone — very special. You really are. You're a one-of-a-kind treasure, one who is so valued not just by me... but by everyone in our whole family.

You have qualities within you that many people would love to have, and those who really and truly know you... are so glad that they do. There are so many marvelous things about you that few ever get to see. You have so many gifts within — those you're only beginning to discover and all the ones you're already aware of.

Never forget what a treasure you are. That special person in the mirror may not always get to hear all the compliments you so sweetly deserve, but
    you are so worthy of
        such an abundance
            ...of thanks and joy and love.

You Are Such a Gift

You have so many moments ahead of you...
Days that will bring new people into your
life and times that will bring new friends
into your world.

Having had the wonderful pleasure of
knowing you (since the minute you were
born!) and appreciating the million and
one things that are so wonderful
about you...

I will always hope that the people
who share your life are
special, insightful people who
realize how lucky they are
to be in the presence
of a present
like you.

Your Happiness Is So Important to Me

As you go through the days of your life, busy with all the responsibilities the world has placed upon you, remember to keep the truly special things in mind.

Keep things in perspective: Work, play, learning, living. Have happiness as a part of your priorities! Be creative and aware and wonderfully alive. Work hard, but know that it's for a reason. The seasons of your life would love for you to be as involved in their everyday passages as you can possibly be. If you can accomplish that, if you can always remember where to find your smile, and if you can stay close to the people who are at the center of your life, you have already traveled a very long way on the road to success...

New journeys await you. Decisions lay ahead,
wondering... what you will do, where you will
go, how you will choose when the choices
are yours.

Remember that good decisions come back to
bless you, over and over again. Work for the
ability to choose wisely, to prosper, to succeed.
Listen with your heart as well as your head, to
the glimmers of truth that provide advice and
inspiration to the hours of your days. And let
those truths take you to beautiful places.

Touch the sky, and in your reach,
    believe, achieve, and aspire.

I hope your tomorrows take you to the summit of
your goals, and your joys take you even higher.

I Am So Proud of You

So many wonderful thoughts go unspoken.

But I don't want this one to. I want you to know what an invaluable part of this world you are. I want you to know that there are times when your light shines brighter than any star. You inspire so much gratitude in those who are so glad to discover that people like you really do exist.

I never want you to lose that light. It is like a ray of sunshine finding a way to break through the clouds and warm up the days with a gift of hope and happiness. It is your blessing to the world.

You Are the Treasures of My Life

I know that the best things
in life don't come with price tags
attached to them. Life's most priceless
things are people and families and the
love that holds them all together.

How can I ever begin to tell you of all
the feelings that are inside of me and of
all the love that is there because of you?
There are things I could tell you every day
and still not say often enough.

But I want you to always remember that

forever and ever
I will have a smile
inside of me
that belongs to you.

May you always have an angel by your side • Watching out for you in all the things you do • Reminding you to keep believing in brighter days • Finding ways for your wishes and dreams to take you to beautiful places • Giving you hope that is as certain as the sun • Giving you the strength of serenity as your guide • May you always have love and comfort and courage • And may you always have an angel by your side •

May you always have an angel by your side • Someone there to catch you if you fall • Encouraging your dreams • Inspiring your happiness • Holding your hand and helping you through it all...

In all of our days, our lives are always changing ⬧ Tears come along as well as smiles ⬧ Along the roads you travel, may the miles be a thousand times more lovely than lonely ⬧ May they give you gifts that never, ever end: someone wonderful to love and a dear friend in whom you can confide ⬧ May you have rainbows after every storm ⬧ May you have hopes to keep you warm ⬧

⬧ And may you always have an angel
by your side ⬧

24 Things to Always Remember...
and One Thing to Never Forget

Your presence is a present to the world.
You're unique and one of a kind.
Your life can be what you want it to be.
Take the days just one at a time.

Count your blessings, not your troubles.
You'll make it through whatever comes along.
Within you are so many answers.
Understand, have courage, be strong.

Don't put limits on yourself.
So many dreams are waiting to be realized.
Decisions are too important to leave to chance.
Reach for your peak, your goal, your prize...

Nothing wastes more energy than worrying.
The longer one carries a problem,
    the heavier it gets.
Don't take things too seriously.
Live a life of serenity, not a life of regrets.

Remember that a little love goes a long way.
Remember that a lot… goes forever.
Remember that friendship is a wise investment.
Life's treasures are people… together.

Realize that it's never too late.
Do ordinary things in an extraordinary way.
Have health and hope and happiness.
Take the time to wish upon a star.

And don't ever forget…
    for even a day… how very special you are.

Thanks for All the Joy
You've Given Me

I want you to know how amazing you are.
I want you to know how much you're
treasured and celebrated and quietly thanked.

I want you to feel really good...
    about who you are.
About all the great things you do!
I want you to appreciate your uniqueness.
Acknowledge your talents and abilities.
Realize what a beautiful soul you have.
Understand the wonder within.

You make so much sun shine through, and you
inspire so much joy in the lives of everyone who
is lucky enough to know you.

You are so special, giving so many
people a reason to smile. You deserve to receive
the best in return, and one of my heart's
favorite hopes is that the happiness you give
away will come back to warm you
        each and every day of your life.

A Keepsake... to Last Forever

And now, before this book comes to a close,
I want to share a special thought that lovingly
goes from my heart... to each of yours.

I want to thank you for giving me the best
memories and the happiest hopes any parent
could ever dream of having. I am so grateful for
your presence in my life, and I always will be.

I hope that you'll keep this book forever and
that — every time you see it in the years
ahead — your lives will be warmed with the glow
of a special reminder... one that makes you smile
just to know how much you're loved and what
wonderful blessings you have always been.

If I were given a chance to be
   anything I wanted to become,
     there's nothing I'd rather be
      than your parent.

     And there's no one
      I'd rather have
       as my children.

About the Author

Douglas Pagels has been a favorite Blue Mountain Arts writer for many years. His philosophical sayings and sentiments on friendship and love have been translated into seven languages and shared with millions of people worldwide in notecards, calendars, and his previous books. He lives in the mountains of Colorado with his wife and two sons.